Charlie Chan's
Words of Wisdom

A collection of 600 proverbs spoken by
the cinema's inscrutable Oriental detective

With twelve pages of rare stills and
pubilicy photos, including scenes
from the "lost" Charlie Chan films.

Mysteries From Wildside Press

Earl Derr Biggers

The Agony Column
Fifty Candles

Michael Bracken

Bad Girls: One Dozen Dangerous Dames
Deadly Campaign
Tequila Sunrise

David Dvorkin

The Cavaradossi Killings
Time for Sherlock Holmes

Joe L. Hensley

Robak's Cross
Robak's Fire
Robak's Firm
A Killing in Gold
The Poison Summer
Song of Corpus Juris
Final Doors
Rivertown Risk
Outcasts

Marvin Kaye

My Brother the Druggist
My Son the Druggist
A Lively Game of Murder
The Soap Opera Slaughters
Bullets for Macbeth
The Country Music Murders

Ray Faraday Nelson

Dog-Headed Death

Hayford Peirce

Trouble in Tahiti: Blood on the Hibiscus
Trouble in Tahiti: Commissaire Tama, Chief of Police
Trouble in Tahiti: P.I. Joe Caneili, Discrétion Assurée

CHARLIE CHAN'S
WORDS OF WISDOM

Howard M. Berlin

Wildside Press
New York • New Jersey • California • Ohio

CHARLIE CHAN'S WORDS OF WISDOM

First Wildside Press edition: June 2001

Wildside Press
P.O. Box 45
Gillette, NJ 07933
www.wildsidepress.com

CONTENTS

INTRODUCTION

Aphorisms are short, pointed sentences expressing a truth or precept. In the movies, the inscrutable Charlie Chan, especially Warner Oland's Chan, was famous for his many pithy pearls of wisdom. These proverbs, sometimes presented as slight variations in wording of other well-known sayings, are perhaps the one most noticeable feature that distinguishes Charlie Chan from the many detectives that appeared on films, even that of Sherlock Holmes. Many of us have come to enjoy these Confucius-like expressions, many of which begin with the requisite "Ancient ancestor once say . . ." and are referred to by some authors as Chanograms, Chanisms, and Biggersisms.

Three books, to various degrees, have compiled these famous proverbial sayings attributed to the Charlie Chan character of the movies. The first was *Quotations from Charlie Chan* (Golden Press, 1968), edited by Harvey Chertok and Martha Torge and which has long been out of print. More than 320 quotations are divided into 36 categories, such as those having reference to wisdom, truth, superstition, love, friends, etc. Unfortunately no indications are provided as to which film a particular quotation is from. Furthermore, the two editors indicated that they obtained their compilation from the screen dialogs of only 21 Charlie Chan films—the Twentieth

Century-Fox inclusive entries from *Charlie Chan in London* (1934) to *Castle in the Desert* (1942) with the exception of *Charlie Chan in Paris* (1935) which was considered "lost" at that time. Also missing from this list of 21 films were the films prior to *Charlie Chan in London*, also considered to be lost then—*Behind That Curtain* (1929), *Charlie Chan Carries On* (1931), *The Black Camel* (1931), *Charlie Chan's Chance* (1932), *Charlie Chan's Greatest Case* (1933), *Charlie Chan's Courage* (1934)—and all 17 Charlie Chan films by Monogram. However, several aphorisms from *Charlie Chan Carries On*, *Charlie Chan's Greatest Case*, and *Charlie Chan's Courage*, based on confirmation of published reviews and other sources, were indeed included in the Chertok-Torge book.

Following the printing of *Quotations from Charlie Chan*, film copies of *"Curtain," "Camel,"* and *"Paris"* have since been found and more than 30 years later, two additional *Charlie Chan* books have been published. The first is *A Guide to Charlie Chan Films* (Greenwood Press, 1999) by Charles P. Mitchell. In this book, Mitchell considers the quotations as falling into to one of the following six categories: direct quotes, paraphrases, metaphors, observations, insults, and jokes. However none of the quotations are individually annotated as such. Instead, at the end of each film's discussion, Mitchell lists the aphorisms of the known *Charlie Chan* films in order of chronological occurrence in the film (presented in alphabetical order), but without any indication to whom these were spoken.

Six months later, my book, *The Charlie Chan Film Encyclopedia* (McFarland, 2000), was released. Here, all the aphorisms (in alphabetical order) are presented as a group. They are listed for each movie (in chronological order) along with to whom the quotation was spoken to. For fans of the *Charlie Chan* films, this format was done to give a better perspective to the proverb's meaning and context.

In all fairness, there will never be a definitive book complete with *all* the famous sayings attributed to the Oriental sleuth, even if all the lost films are eventually accounted for. There are some individuals who feel that virtually every line uttered by Charlie Chan is profound. However, some of the more obvious sayings have not been included in this book because they are so specific to the moment that, when taken out of context of the particular film, its meaning is lost. Until those from the four films currently considered lost—*Charlie Chan Carries On, Charlie Chan's Chance, Charlie Chan's Greatest Case*, and *Charlie Chan's Courage*—are found, one can only rely on those obtained from published reviews or available scripts. In the *Charlie Chan Film Encyclopedia*, I include quotations that were not included in Mitchell's book and he has a number that I previously overlooked. Also, we both have quotations that are not present in the Chertok-Torge book and who have almost 80 sayings that cannot be attributed to any particular film of the *Charlie Chan* series.

In preparing this book, I again reviewed copies of all the 41 available *Charlie Chan* (talkie) films from my own collection and the reviews from the *New York Times* for the four lost films. I recompiled the quotations from these three books, attributing each quotation to the particular film and, within parentheses, indicated to whom the proverb is spoken. However, aphorisms spoken by those other than Charlie Chan character are not included. In deciding on the format for presentation in this book, I settled on a combination of formats from both my book and Mitchell's: each film, in chronological order, is presented with its aphorisms in the order they occur in the film. Also, I noted to whom the quotation was directed. Those complied for each of the four lost films, using published reviews and other sources, are simply listed in alphabetical order. As a result, only one film, *Behind That Curtain*, had no aphorisms because the role of Charlie Chan (portrayed by E.L. Park) was a minor one, lasting only a few minutes. As many of the 36 categories of the Chertok-Torge book in my opinion are very subjective, I decided against following this arrangement.

In addition to the listing of Charlie Chan's aphorisms, I have also included two other items associated with *Charlie Chan* film series. First are the words to a song about Princess Ming Lo Fu, a Chinese children's lullaby sung by Charlie Chan in *Charlie Chan in Shanghai* (1935). Also included is the text of a promotional short starring Warner Oland as an endorsement for a 1935 referendum in Pennsylvania to allow theaters to show movies on Sundays.

Besides the popular *Charlie Chan* films made by Twentieth Century-Fox and Monogram, two other Oriental detective film series were contemporaneously made. One is the *Mr. Moto* series (8 films, Twentieth Century-Fox, 1937–1939) starring Peter Lorre, and the other is the *Mr. Wong* series (6 films, Monogram, 1938–1940) featuring Boris Karloff for the first five and Keye Luke for the last entry. The few wise sayings that can be attributed to these two series are also included in this book.

In all, there are over 600 words of wisdom attributed to these three Oriental detectives. Unlike Mitchell's *A Guide to Charlie Chan Films*, I do not include those from *The Return of Charlie Chan* (1971) with Ross Martin; the 1957 TV series, *The New Adventures of Charlie Chan* starring J. Carrol Naish; the Peter Ustinov spoof, *Charlie Chan and the Curse of the Dragon Queen* (1981); or any of the few foreign language films, such as *Eran Trece* (1931, Spanish), a remake of *Charlie Chan Carries On*.

For the record, my favorite aphorism is, "Mind like parachute—only function when open!" (from *Charlie Chan at the Circus*), which I often place at the beginning of exams in many of the college courses I teach. I hope you enjoy this little book as much as I had fun compiling it.

As Charlie Chan often says, "Thank you, so much."

Dr. Howard M. Berlin
Wilmington, Delaware

CHARLIE CHAN

Inspector Charlie Chan of the Honolulu Police Department is a rotund Chinese detective created by Earl Derr Biggers. Biggers modeled Chan after the real-life Chinese detective, Chang Apana, who lived with his large family in Honolulu on Punchbowl Hill, and is the most prolific detective to appear on film with the exception of Sherlock Holmes.

From the original silent film *The House Without a Key* (1925) to the series' finale, *The Sky Dragon* in 1949, none of the six actors who were to play Charlie were Chinese. In the three earliest films, where Charlie Chan was not even the main character, two actors were Japanese (George Kuwa and Kamiyama Sojin in the silent films) and one was British (E.L. Park, although some think he was Korean, in the first Chan talkie). For the movie series that began its run in 1931, none of the Chan actors was even Oriental. One actor was Swedish (Warner Oland) and two were Americans (Sidney Toler and Roland Winters).

Charlie Chan's physical attributes were not typical of most movie detectives and he often relied on a mixture of brains, good manners, and charm to solve many of his murder cases. With the three actors in the role of Charlie Chan as the film's main character, there evolved three distinct interpretations of Chan's character. Because many of the films featured one or more Charlie Chan's ever-present children, it is not surprising then that most of the well-celebrated aphorisms are directed at them.

Warner Oland as Charlie Chan

Warner Oland is perhaps the best-known and best-liked of the actors who portrayed Charlie Chan. He was born Johan Värner Ölund in the small Swedish village of Nyby. Although born to Swedish and Russian parents, a previous Mongol presence in Sweden provided Oland with uncanny but natural features that suited the portrayals of Orientals when a mustache and beard were added.

In the 16 Oland Chans, Charlie is a humble, polite policeman with the Honolulu Police Department, but rarely does he do any actual work for them. Instead, he usually pops up in various locales around the world such as London, Paris, Egypt, Shanghai, Berlin, New York, Monte Carlo, Reno, Panama, and Rio. The one notable exception is *The Black Camel* (1931) which was filmed entirely on location in Honolulu, although there were other films would have Charlie start out from Honolulu. In the Fox films made before *Charlie Chan in London* (1934), Charlie is generally left alone to solve the cases, is more energetic in tracking the culprits, and often uses himself as bait in catching the murderer. With the *London* entry, Chan now begins to adopt a more methodical approach by gathering all the suspects that are still alive for the reconstruction of the crime.

Very often in public, Oland would talk in the stilted speech pattern and used mannerisms that were associated with his Charlie Chan characterization. He would quote sayings that he used in the films and often referred to himself as "humble father," giving many the impression that he actually thought *he was* Charlie Chan. Oland made 16 films as Charlie Chan.

Warner Oland (1931–1938)

Charlie Chan Filmography
Warner Oland

Charlie Chan Carries On (1931)

I *The Black Camel* (1931)

Charlie Chan's Chance (1932)

Charlie Chan's Greatest Case (1933)

Charlie Chan's Courage (1934)

2 X *Charlie Chan in London* (1934)

2x *Charlie Chan in Paris* (1935)

2x *Charlie Chan in Egypt* (1935)

2x *Charlie Chan in Shanghai* (1935)

I *Charlie Chan's Secret* (1936)

I *Charlie Chan at the Circus* (1936)

I *Charlie Chan at the Race Track* (1936)

I *Charlie Chan at the Opera* (1936)

I *Charlie Chan at the Olympics* (1937)

I *Charlie Chan on Broadway* (1937)

I *Charlie Chan at Monte Carlo* (1937)

Charlie Chan Carries On (1931)

[As obtained from published sources and reviews]

Marguerite Churchill . . . . Pamela Potter
John Garrick . . . . Mark Kennaway
Warner Oland . . . . Charlie Chan
Warren Hymer . . . . Max Minchin
Marjorie White . . . . Sadie Minchin
C. Henry Gordon . . . . . John Ross, alias for Jim Everhard
William Holden . . . . Patrick Tail
George Brent . . . . Capt. Ronald Keane
Peter Gawthorne . . . . Inspector Duff
John T. Murray . . . . Dr. Lofton
John Swor . . . . Elmer Benbow
Goodee Montgomery . . . . Mrs. Benbow
Jason Robards . . . . Walter Honeywood
Lumsden Hare . . . . Inspector Hanley
Zeffie Tilbury . . . . Mrs. Luce
Betty Francisco . . . . Sybil Conway
Harry Beresford . . . . Kent
John Rogers . . . . Martin
J. Gunnis Davis . . . . Eben

- *A big head is only a good place for a big headache.*

- *Advice after mistake is like medicine after dead man's funeral. (Inspector Duff and Pamela Potter)*

- *All mischief begins with the opening of one's mouth.*

- *Ancient proverbs must not be taken too literally.*

- *Each man think own cuckoos better than next man's nightingales. (Inspector Duff)*

- *Good wife best household furniture. (Mark Kennaway)*

- *He who feeds the chicken deserves the egg.*

- *Man seldom scratches where does not itch. (Patrick Tait)*

- *Man should never hurry except when going to catch flea.*

- *Only very brave mouse make nest in cat's ear. (Inspector Duff and Pamela Potter)*

- *Time does not press, and talk will not cook rice. (Captain Keane)*

- *Too late to dig well after honorable house is on fire. (Mrs. Chan)*

The Black Camel (1931)

Warner Oland	Charlie Chan
Sally Eilers	Julie O'Neill
Béla Lugosi	Tarneverro, alias for Arthur Mayo
Dorothy Revier	Shelah Fane
Victor Varconi	Robert Fyfe
Murray Kinnell	Smith
William Post	Alan Jaynes
Robert Young	Jimmy Bradshaw
Violet Dunn	Anna, alias for Mrs. Denny Mayo
J. M. Kerrigan	Thomas MacMasters
Mary Gordon	Mrs. MacMasters
Rita Rozelle	Luana
Otto Yamaoka	Kashimo
Dwight Frye	Jessop
Richard Tucker	Wilkie Ballou
Marjorie White	Rita Ballou
C. Henry Gordon	Van Horn

- *Wages of stupidity is hunt for new job. (Kashimo)*

- *Mouse cannot cast shadow like elephant. (Tarneverro)*

- *Always harder to keep murder secret than for egg to bounce on sidewalk. (Tarneverro)*

- *Very few after-dinner speeches equipped with self-stopper. (Tarneverro)*

- *All foxes come at last to fur store. (Tarneverro)*

- *Sometimes difficult to pick up pumpkin with one finger. (Tarneverro)*

- *Death is a black camel that kneels unbidden at every gate. Tonight, black camel has knelt here. (Willkie Ballou)*

- *Alibi have habit of disappearing like hole in water. (Alan Jaynes)*
- *Even bagpipe will not speak when stomach is empty. (the Chief of Police)*
- *Way to find rabbit's residence is to turn rabbit loose, and watch. (Tarneverro)*
- *Always happens—when conscience tries to speak, telephone out of order. (Tarneverro)*
- *Secret of this case harder to determine than alley cat's grandfather. (Kashimo)*
- *Even wisest man sometimes mistake bumble bee for blackbird. (Tarneverro)*
- *Soap and water never can change perfume of Billy goat. (Kashimo)*
- *Only very clever man can bite pie without breaking crust. (Julie O'Neil and Jimmy Bradshaw)*
- *Learn from hen. Never boast about egg until after egg's birthday. (Jimmy Bradshaw)*
- *Can cut off monkey's tail, but he is still monkey. (Kashimo)*

Charlie Chan's Chance (1932)

[As obtained from published sources and reviews]

Warner Oland	Charlie Chan
Alexander Kirkland	John R. Douglas
H. B. Warner	Inspector Fife
Marian Nixon	Shirley Marlowe
Linda Watkins	Gloria Garland
James Kirkwood	Inspector Flannery
Ralph Morgan	Barry Kirk
James Todd	*Kenneth Dunwood*, alias for *Alan Raleigh*
Herbert Bunston	*Garrick Enderly*
James Wang	*Kee Lin*
Joe Brown	*Doctor*
Charles McNaughton	Paradise
Edward Peil, Sr.	Li Gung

- *Even wise fly sometimes mistake spider web for old man's whiskers.*

- *It is as difficult as trying to pick up needle with boxing glove.*

- *My day's work has been useless as life preserver for fish.*

- *Some heads like hard nuts—much better if well cracked.*

- *This is as unexpected as squirt from aggressive grapefruit.*

Charlie Chan's Greatest Case (1933)

[As obtained from published sources and reviews]

Warner Oland	Charlie Chan
Heather Angel	Carlotta Eagan
Roger Imhof	The beachcomber
John Warburton	John Quincy Winterslip
Walter Byron	Harry Jennison
Ivan Simpson	T.M. Brade
Virginia Cherrill	Barbara Winterslip
Francis Ford	Captain Hallett
Robert Warwick	Dan Winterslip
Frank McGlynn	Amos Winterslip
Clara Blandick	Minerva Winterslip
Claude E. King	Captain Arthur Temple Cope
William Slack	James Eagan
Gloria Roy	Arlene Compton
Cornelius Keefe	Steve Leatherbee

- *Cat which tries to catch two mice at one time goes without supper.*

- *Make haste only when withdrawing hand from mouth of tiger.*

- *Only facts and motives lead to a murderer.*

- *Only make haste when catching flea.*

- *Theories like fingerprints—everybody has them.*

Charlie Chan's Courage (1934)

[As obtained from published sources and reviews]

Warner Oland . . . . Charlie Chan, alias Ah Kim
Drue Leyton . . . . Paula Graham
Donald Woods . . . . Bob Crawford
Paul Harvey . . . . J. P. Madden/Jerry Delaney
Murray Kinnell . . . . Martin Thorne
Reginald Mason . . . . Alexander Crawford
Virginia Hammond . . . . Sally Jordan
Si Jenks . . . . Will Holley
Harvey Clark . . . . Professor Gamble
Jerry Jerome . . . . "Shaky" Phil Maydorf
Jack Carter . . . . Victor Jordan
James Wang . . . . Louie Wong
DeWitt C. Jennings . . . . Sergeant Brackett
Francis Ford . . . . Hewitt
Lucilie Miller . . . . Stenographer
Mary McLaren . . . . Mother
Gail Kaye . . . . Child
Larry Fisher . . . . Taxi driver
Sam McDaniels . . . . Porter
Carl Stockdale . . . . Station lounger
Lila Chevret, Susan Fleming . . . . . Chorus girls
Caryl Lincoln . . . . Leading lady
John David Horsley . . . . Leading man
George Magrill . . . . Heavy
Frank Mills . . . . Prop man
Sherry Hall . . . . Assistant director
James P. Burtis . . . . Eddie Boston
Paul McVey . . . . Director
Wade Boteler . . . . Capt. Bliss
Teru Shimada . . . . Jujitsu man

- *Anxious man hurries too fast—often stubs big toe.*
- *Hunting needle in haystack only requires careful inspection of hay.*
- *Large sugar bowl temps many flies.*
- *Tread softly. Beg to recall that sitting hen squats cautiously on thin eggs.*

Charlie Chan in London (1934)

Warner Oland . . . . Inspector Charlie Chan
Drue Leyton. . . . . Pamela Gray
Raymond Milland . . . . Neil Howard
Mona Barrie . . . . Lady Mary Bristol
Alan Mowbray . . . . Geoffrey Richmond, alias for Paul Frank
Murray Kinnell . . . . . . Phillips, alias for Capt. Seeton
Douglas Walton . . . . Hugh Gray
Walter Johnson . . . . Jerry Gorton
E.E. Clive . . . . Detective Sergeant Thacker
George Barraud . . . . Major Jardine
Madge Bellamy . . . . Mrs. Becky Fothergill
David Torrence . . . . . Home Secretary Sir Lionel Bashford
John Rogers. . . . . Lake
Paul England . . . . Bunny Fothergill
Elsa Buchanan . . . . Alice Rooney
Perry Ivins . . . . Kemp

- *Front seldom tell truth. To know occupants of house, always look in back yard. (Sir Lionel Bashford)*

- *Every front has back. (Sir Lionel Bashford)*

- *No time to expose lies—must expose truth. (Geoffrey Richmond)*

- *Murder not very good joke—quite unfunny. (Sgt. Thacker)*

- *Case like inside of radio—many connections, not all related. (Geoffrey Richmond)*

- *When death enters window, no time for life to go by door. (Geoffrey Richmond)*

- *If you want wild bird to sing—do not put him in cage. (Sgt. Thacker)*

Charlie Chan in Paris (1935)

Warner Oland . . . . Charlie Chan
Mary Brian . . . . Yvette Lamartine
Thomas Beck . . . . Victor Descartes
Erik Rhodes . . . . Max Corday
John Miljan . . . . Albert Dufresne
Murray Kinnell . . . . Henri Latouche
Minor Watson . . . . Inspector Renard
John Qualen . . . . Concierge
Keye Luke . . . . Lee Chan
Henry Kolker . . . . Paul Lamartine
Dorothy Appleby . . . . Nardi
Ruth Peterson . . . . Renee Jacquard
Perry Ivins . . . . Bedell

- *It is always good fortune to give alms upon entering a city. (Marcel Xavier)*

- *Young bird must learn to fly. (Victor Descartes)*

- *Youth tonic for old blood. (Yvette Lamartine)*

- *Mud turtle in pond more safe than man on horseback. (Yvette Lamartine)*

- *Joy in heart more enjoyable than bullet. (Lee Chan)*

- *Good detective never ask what and why, until after he see. (Lee Chan)*

- *Kindness in heart better than gold in bank. (Henri Latouche)*

- *Must turn up many stones to find hiding place of snake. (Paul Lamartine)*

- *Important fox must not know hounds pursue. (Lee Chan)*

- *Only foolish man waste words when argument is lost. (Inspector Renard)*

- *Perfect case like perfect doughnut—has hole. Optimist only sees doughnut—pessimist sees hole. (Inspector Renard)*

- *Silence big sister to wisdom. (Yvette Lamartine)*

- *Hasty conclusion like gunpowder—easy to explode. (Inspector Renard)*

- *Little keyhole big friend to stupid detective. (Max Corday)*

- *Eyes of kitten open only after nine days. (Lee Chan)*

- *Very difficult to explain hole in doughnut, but hole always there. (Inspector Renard)*

- *Canary bird out of cage may fly far. (Henri Latouche)*

- *Faith is best foundation for happy future. (Victor Descartes)*

- *Cannot see contents of nut until shell is cracked. (Victor Descartes)*

- *Man cannot drink from glass without touching. (Victor Descartes)*

- *Grain of sand in eye may hide mountain. (Victor Descartes)*

Charlie Chan in Egypt (1935)

Warner Oland . . . . Charlie Chan
Pat Paterson . . . . Carol Arnold
Thomas Beck . . . . Tom Evans
Rita Cansino . . . . Nayda
Stepin Fetchit . . . . Snowshoes
Jameson Thomas . . . . Dr. Anton Racine
Frank Conroy . . . . Professor John Thurston
Nigel De Brulier . . . . Edfu Ahmad
James Eagles . . . . Barry Arnold
Paul Porcasi . . . . Fuad Soueida
Arthur Stone . . . . Dragoman
John George . . . . Ali, gravedigger who dies
Frank Reicher . . . . Dr. Jaipur
George Irving . . . . Professor Arnold
Anita Brown . . . . Snowshoes' friend
John Davidson . . . . Daoud Atrash, chemist

- *Drop of plain water on thirsty tongue more precious than gold in purse. (Snowshoes)*

- *Reverence for ancestors most commendable. (Snowshoes)*

- *Insignificant molehill sometimes more important than conspicuous mountain. (Tom Evans and Carol Arnold)*

- *Waiting for tomorrow waste of today. (Tom Evans)*

- *Cannot read printing in new book until pages cut. (Police Chief Soueida)*

- *Theory like mist on eyeglasses—obscures facts. (Dr. Racine)*

- *Impossible to prepare defense until direction of attack is known. (John Thurston)*

- *Story of man very short. Life. Death. (Tom Evans)*

- *Am reminded of ancient saying, "From life to death is reach of man." (Tom Evans)*

- *Hasty conclusion easy to make—like hole in water. (Tom Evans)*

- *Kind thoughts add favorable weight in balance of life and death. (Nayda)*

- *Admitting failure, like drinking bitter tea. (Carol Arnold)*

- *Courage greatest devotion to those we love. (Carol Arnold)*

- *Journey of life like feather on stream—must continue with current. (Snowshoes)*

Charlie Chan in Shanghai (1936)

Warner Oland . . . . Charlie Chan
Irene Hervey . . . . Diana Woodland
Charles Locher . . . . Philip Nash
Russell Hicks . . . . James Andrews
Keye Luke . . . . Lee Chan
Halliwell Hobbes . . . . . . Chief of Police Col. Watkins
Frederik Vogeding . . . . Ivan Marloff
Neil Fitzgerald . . . . Dakin
Max Wagner . . . . Taxi driver

- *Holiday mood like fickle girl—privilege to change mind. (reporters)*

- *Old excuse, like ancient Billy goat—has whiskers. (Lee Chan)*

- *Two ears for every tongue. (Sir Stanley Woodland)*

- *Motive like end of string, tied in many knots. End may be in sight but hard to unravel. (Col. Watkins)*

- *Only one enemy necessary to commit murder. (Col. Watkins)*

- *Talk cannot cook rice. (Lee Chan)*

- *Silence best answer when uncertain. (Lee Chan)*

- *Distance no hindrance to fond thoughts. (picture of family at bedside)*

- *Dreams like liars—distort facts. (Lee Chan)*

- *Cold omelet like fish out of sea—does not improve with age. (Lee Chan)*

- *If answer known, question seem unnecessary. (Ivan Marloff)*

- *Hasty conclusion like hind leg of mule—kick backward. (Ivan Marloff)*

- *Beauty of poppy conceal sting of death. (James Andrews)*

- *Spider does not spin web for single fly. (James Andrews)*

- *Long journey always start with one short step. (James Andrews)*

- *Owner of face cannot always see nose. (Col. Watkins)*

- *Shot in dark sometimes find eye of bull. (Lee Chan)*

- *Innocent man does not run away. (Col. Watkins)*

- *Smart rats know when to leave ship. (James Andrews)*

- *Only foolish dog pursue flying bird. (James Andrews)*

- *Soothing drink, like summer shower, bring grateful relief. (James Andrews)*

- *Appearances sometimes deceiving—like wolf in lamb's clothing. (James Andrews)*

- *No one knows less about servants than the master. (James Andrews)*

- *Give you plenty of rope, you make excellent noose for neck. (James Andrews)*

Charlie Chan's Secret (1936)

Warner Oland . . . . Charlie Chan
Rosina Lawrence . . . . Alice Lowell
Charles Quigley . . . . Dick Williams
Henrietta Crossman . . . . Henrietta Lowell
Edward Trevor . . . . Fred Gage
Astrid Allwyn . . . . Janice Gage
Herbert Mundin . . . . Baxter
Jonathan Hale . . . . Warren T. Phelps
Egon Brecher . . . . Ulrich
Gloria Roy . . . . Carlotta
Ivan Miller . . . . Morton
Arthur Edmund Carewe . . . . . . Professor Bowan

- *Mysterious shadows of night cling to old house like moss on tombstone. (Baxter)*

- *Greetings at end of journey like refreshing rain after long drought. (Henrietta Lowell)*

- *Best place for skeleton is in family closet. (Dick Williams and Fred Gage)*

- *Most fortunate gift to be able to cross bridge to dwelling place of honorable ancestors before arriving. (Professor Bowen and Carlotta)*

- *If strength were all, tiger would not fear scorpion. (Dick Williams and Inspector Morton)*

- *Fingerprints very valuable if detective can catch owners of fingers. (Fingerprint technician)*

- *Perhaps woman's intuition, like feather on arrow—may help flight to truth. (Henrietta Lowell)*

- *Boy Scout knife, like lady's hairpin (hat pin), have many uses. (Henrietta Lowell)*

- *Necessity is mother of invention but sometimes stepmother of deception. (Henrietta Lowell)*

- *When pilot unreliable—ship cannot keep true course. (Henrietta Lowell)*

- *Role of dead man require very little acting. (Baxter)*

- *Finding web of spider does not prove which spider spin web. (Henrietta Lowell)*

- *Punch in ribs more desirable than shot in back. (Henrietta Lowell)*

- *So sorry, like child who play with matches—get burned. (Inspector Morton)*

- *Wheel of fate has many spokes. (Dick Williams)*

- *When weaving net—all threads counted. (Janice Gage)*

- *Unknown danger like summer lightning—strike where least expected. (Dick Williams)*

- *Hasty deduction like ancient egg—look good from outside. (Baxter)*

- *With proper lever, baby's fingers can move mountain. (Inspector Morton)*

Charlie Chan at the Circus (1936)

Warner Oland . . . . Charlie Chan
Keye Luke . . . . Lee Chan
George Brasno. . . . . Colonel Tim
Olive Brasno . . . . Lady Tiny
Francis Ford. . . . . John Gaines
Maxine Reiner . . . . Marie Norman
John McGuire . . . . Hal Blake
Shirley Deane . . . . Louise Norman
Paul Stanton. . . . . Joe Kinney
J. Carrol Naish . . . . Tom Holt
Boothe Howard . . . . Dan Farrell
Drue Leyton. . . . . Nellie Ferrell
Wade Boteler . . . . Lt. Macy
Shia Jung . . . . Su Toy

- *Free ticket to circus like gold ring on merry-go-round—make enjoyment double. (Joe Kinney)*

- *Size of package does not indicate quality within. (Lady Tiny and Colonel Tim)*

- *Curiosity responsible for cat needing nine lives. (Lee Chan)*

- *More than one way to remove skin from cat. (Mr. Gaines)*

- *Much evil can enter through very small space. (Mr. Gaines)*

- *One ounce of experience worth ton of detective books. (Lee Chan)*

- *Man who seek trouble never find it far off. (Lady Tiny)*

- *Frightened bird very difficult to catch. (Lt. Macy)*

- *Give man plenty of rope—will hang self. (Lt. Macy)*

- *Guilty conscience only enemy to peaceful rest. (Mr. Gaines)*
- *Circus performer, like detective, must be Johnny of many trades. (Holt)*
- *Ancient adage say, "Music soothe savage breast." (Lee Chan)*
- *Question without answer like far away water—no good for nearby fire. (Holt)*
- *Enemy who misses mark, like serpent, must coil to strike again. (Lt. Macy)*
- *Very wise to know way out before going in. (Lee Chan)*
- *Very easy to read mind when clue like rag on sore thumb. (Lady Tiny)*
- *Facts like photographic film—must be exposed before developing. (Tiny and Tim)*
- *Trouble rain on man already wet. (Lady Tiny)*
- *Too soon to count chickens until eggs are in nest. (Lt. Macy)*
- *One grain of luck sometimes worth more than whole rice field of wisdom. (Lt. Macy)*
- *Cannot tell where path lead until reach end of road. (Lt. Macy)*
- *Evidence like nose on anteater. (Lee Chan)*
- *Good tools shorten labor. (Lee Chan)*
- *Inquisitive person like bear after honey—sometimes find hornet's nest. (Lt. Macy)*
- *Best to slip with foot than with tongue. (Lee Chan)*
- *Silent witness sometimes speak loudest. (Lt. Macy)*
- *Magnifying female charms very ancient optical illusion. (Lee Chan)*
- *Even if name signed one million times—no two signatures exactly alike. (Lt. Macy)*

- *Not always wise to accept simplest solution. (Lt. Macy)*
- *Mind like parachute—only function when open. (Lt. Macy)*
- *Unloaded gun always cause most trouble. (Holt)*
- *No use to hurry unless sure of catching right train. (Lt. Macy)*

Charlie Chan at the Race Track (1936)

Warner Oland. . . . . Charlie Chan
Keye Luke . . . . Lee Chan
Helen Wood . . . . Alice Fenton
Thomas Beck . . . . Bruce Rogers
Alan Dinehart . . . . George Chester
Gavin Muir . . . . Bagley
Gloria Roy . . . . Catherine Chester
Jonathan Hale . . . . Warren Fenton
G. P. Huntley, Jr. . . . . Denny Barton
George Irving . . . . Major Gordon Kent
Frank Coghlan, Jr. . . . . Eddie Brill
Frankie Darro . . . . "Tip" Collins
John Rogers . . . . Mooney
John H. Allen . . . . "Streamline" Jones
Harry Jans . . . . Al Meers

- *Record indicate most murder result from violence, and murder without bloodstains like Amos without Andy—most unusual. (Policemen in squadroom)*

- *Smart fly keep out of gravy. (Lee Chan)*

- *When player cannot see man who deal cards—much wiser to stay out of game. (Lee Chan)*

- *Suspicion often father of truth. (Charlie Chan's Chief of Police)*

- *Easy to criticize—most difficult to be correct. (Warren Fenton)*

- *Frequent spanking when young, make rear view very familiar. (Lee Chan)*

- *Confucius say, "No man is poor who have worthy son." (Lee Chan)*

- *Hasty conclusion like toy balloon—easy blow up, easy pop. (Lee Chan)*

- *Surprise attack often find enemy unprepared. (Lee Chan)*

- *Long road sometimes shortest way to end of journey. (Warren and Alice Fenton)*

- *Foolish to seek fortune when real treasure hiding under nose. (Alice Fenton)*

- *Rabbit run very fast but sometimes turtle win race. (George Chester)*

- *Ocean have many fish. (Lee Chan)*

- *Foolish rooster who stick head in lawn mower end in stew. (Lee Chan)*

- *Innocent grass may conceal snake. (Race track guard)*

- *Man who flirt with dynamite sometimes fly with angels. (Lee Chan)*

- *Roots of tree laid in many directions. (Lee Chan)*

- *Man with gun like lightning—never strike twice in same place. (Lee Chan)*

- *Useless talk like boat without oar—get no place. (Lee Chan)*

- *Cold-blooded murder no joke. (George Chester)*

- *Truth sometimes like stab of cruel knife. (Catherine Chester)*

- *Good wife best household furniture." (Bruce Rogers and Alice Fenton)*

Charlie Chan at the Opera (1936)

Warner Oland . . . . Charlie Chan
Boris Karloff . . . . Gravelle
Keye Luke . . . . Lee Chan
Charlotte Henry . . . . Mlle. Kitty Rochelle
Thomas Beck . . . . Phil Childers
Margaret Irving . . . . Mme. Lilli Rochelle
Gregory Gaye . . . . Enrico Barelli
Nedda Harrington . . . . Mme. Anita Barelli
Frank Conroy . . . . Mr. Whitely
Guy Usher . . . . Inspector Regan
William Demarest . . . . Sergeant Kelly
Maurice Cass . . . . Mr. Arnold
Tom McGuire . . . . Morris

- *Humble father once say, "Politeness golden key that open many doors." (Sgt. Kelly and Inspector Regan)*

- *Confucius say, "Luck happy combination of foolish accidents." (Sgt. Kelly and Inspector Regan)*

- *Small things sometimes tell large stories. (Inspector Regan)*

- *Madame's voice, like monastery bell, when ringing, must attend. (Madame Rochelle)*

- *Puppy love very expensive pastime. (Lee Chan)*

- *Roses in romance, like tenor in opera—sing most persuasive love song. (Owner of flower shop)*

- *Dead hands cannot hide knife. (Inspector Regan)*

- *Humility only defense against rightful blame. (Inspector Regan)*

- *Voice from back seat sometime very disconcerting to driver. (Mr. Whitely)*

- *Man who ride on merry-go-round often enough finally catch brass ring. (Lee Chan)*

- *Very old Chinese wise man once say, "Madness twin brother of genius, because each live in world created by own ego—one sometimes mistaken for other." (Gravelle)*

- *Ancient proverb mean, "When fear attack brain, tongue wave distress signal." (Sgt. Kelly)*

Charlie Chan at the Olympics (1936)

Warner Oland . . . . Charlie Chan
Katherine DeMille . . . . Yvonne Roland
Pauline Moore . . . . Betty Adams
Allan Lane . . . . Richard Masters
Keye Luke . . . . Lee Chan
C. Henry Gordon . . . . Arthur Hughes
John Eldredge . . . . Cartwright
Layne Tom, Jr. . . . . Charlie Chan, Jr.
Jonathan Hale . . . . Mr. Hopkins
Morgan Wallace . . . . . . Honorable Charles Zaraka
Frederick Vogeding . . . . . Captain Inspector Strasser
Andrew Tombes . . . . Police Chief Scott
Howard C. Hickman . . . . Dr. Burton

- *Piece of string with hook on one end—optimist on other. (Dr. Burton and Chief Scott in answer to what kind of fishing line Chan prefers)*

- *Good fisherman, like clever merchant, knows lure of bright colors. (Charlie Jr.)*

- *Would be greatest blessing if all war fought with machinery instead of human beings. (Charlie Jr.)*

- *Fish in sea like tick on dog—always present but difficult to catch. (Charlie Jr.)*

- *Truth like football—receive many kicks before reaching goal. (Mr. Hopkins)*

- *Race not always won by man who start first. (Chief Scott)*

- *Good hunter never warn tiger of trap. (Mr. Hopkins and Cartwright)*

- *Useless to sprinkle salt on tail of time. (Mr. Hopkins)*

- *All play and no work make Charlie Chan very dull policeman. (Arthur Hughes)*

- *Last step eases toil of most difficult journey. (Mr. Hopkins and Cartwright)*

- *Hasty accusation like long shot on horse race—odds good but chances doubtful. (Mr. Hopkins and Cartwright)*

- *When all players hold suspicious cards, good idea to have joker up sleeve. (Lee Chan)*

- *Envelope like skin of banana—must be removed to digest contents. (Lee Chan)*

- *Have never met Santa Claus either yet accept gift from same. (Lee Chan)*

- *Could not be more clear if magnified by two hundred-inch telescope. (Charles Zaraka)*

- *Player sometimes disregard even most expert coaching from sidelines. (Charles Zaraka)*

- *Ancient Chinese philosopher say, "Hope is sunshine which illuminate darkest paths." (Inspector Strasser)*

- *Wise philosopher once say, "Only foolish man will not acknowledge defeat." (Charles Zaraka and Yvonne Roland)*

- *Danger like red light on end of moving train—now safely past. (Lee Chan)*

- *Better for Oriental to lose life than to lose face. (Lee Chan)*

- *Good idea not to accept gold medal until race is won. (Lee Chan)*

Charlie Chan on Broadway (1937)

Warner Oland	Charlie Chan
Keye Luke	Lee Chan
Joan Marsh	Joan Wendall
J. Edward Bromberg	Murdock
Douglas Fowley	Johnny Burke
Harold Huber	Inspector Nelson
Donald Wood	Speed Patten
Louise Henry	Billie Bronson
Joan Woodbury	Marie Collins
Leon Ames	Buzz Moran
Marc Lawrence	Thomas Mitchell
Tashia Mori	Ling Tse
Charles Williams	Meeker
Eugene Borden	Louie

- *Etiquette ignored when lady in distress. (Billie Bronson)*

- *One cabin too small for two detectives. (Lee Chan)*

- *Will feel like sparrow perched on limb with peacocks. (Speed Patten and Inspector Nelson)*

- *New York like mouth of great river—many reefs in channel to break small sightseeing boat from Honolulu. (Lee Chan)*

- *Camera remember many things human eye forget. (Inspector Nelson)*

- *Position of body sometimes gives solution of murder. (Inspector Nelson)*

- *Missing key may fit door to solution. (Inspector Nelson)*

- *Mud of bewilderment now beginning to clear from pool of thought. (Inspector Nelson)*

- *No poison more deadly than ink. (Lee Chan and Inspector Nelson)*

- *Regret slow progress of thought but rejoice at final arrival. (Lee Chan and Inspector Nelson)*

- *Murder case like revolving door—when one side closed, other side open. (Inspector Nelson and Murdock)*

- *Puppy detective perhaps now realize snooping very dangerous business. (Lee Chan)*

- *Triangle very ancient motive for murder. (Marie Collins and Johnny Burke)*

- *To know forgery, one must have original. (Speed Patten)*

Charlie Chan at Monte Carlo (1937)

Warner Oland . . . . Charlie Chan
Keye Luke . . . . Lee Chan
Virginia Field . . . . Evelyn Grey
Sidney Blackmer . . . . Victor Karnoff
Harold Huber . . . . Inspector Jules Joubert
Kay Linaker . . . . Joan Karnoff
Robert Kent . . . . Gordon Chase
Edward Raquello . . . . Paul Savarin
George Lynn . . . . Albert Rogers
Louis Mercier . . . . Taxi driver
George Davis . . . . Pepite
John Bleifer . . . . Ludwig
Georges Renavent . . . . Renault

- *Humble presence no more important than one drop of rain in cloudburst. (Inspector Joubert)*

- *Talk is cheap. (Inspector Joubert)*

- *Illustrious ancestor once say, "Destination is never reached by turning back on same." (Lee Chan)*

- *Fortunately, assassination of French language not serious crime. (Lee Chan)*

- *In future, remember that tongue often hang man quicker than rope. (Lee Chan)*

- *Present case like too many cocktails—make very bad headache. (Inspector Joubert)*

- *Very doubtful petty larceny mouse attack millionaire lion. (Inspector Joubert)*

- *Questions are keys to door of truth. (Inspector Joubert)*

- *Truth cannot be insult. (Victor Karnoff)*
- *Car with new spark plug like flea on new puppy dog—make both most active. (Inspector Joubert)*

Sidney Toler as Charlie Chan

When Sidney Toler took over the role after Oland's death, the character now is one of a sharper-tongued, less patient Chan who uses less physical action than Oland did. As a crime solver, Chan is helping the U.S. government as a Secret Service agent, such as in *Charlie Chan in Panama* (1940). Beginning with *Charlie Chan in the Secret Service* (1944), Charlie now works full time for the U.S. government, fighting enemy spies, which reflected America's participation in World War II.

With a few exceptions, Toler exclusively played the Charlie Chan role 22 times. In 1942, Twentieth Century-Fox had decided the end the series with *Castle in the Desert*. Toler then obtained the rights to the character from Earl Derr Biggers' widow and made 11 more *Charlie Chan* films at Monogram before he died. Compared with Oland, Toler's characterization of Charlie Chan was a more abrasive character who was more of a bully and is often reflected in the aphorisms.

Sidney Toler (1938–1947)

Charlie Chan Filmography
Sidney Toler

1 *Charlie Chan in Honolulu* (1938)

1 *Charlie Chan in Reno* (1939)

1 *Charlie Chan at Treasure Island* (1939)

1 *City in Darkness* (1939)

1 *Charlie Chan in Panama* (1940)

2 *Charlie Chan's Murder Cruise* (1940)

1 *Charlie Chan at the Wax Museum* (1940)

2 *Murder Over New York* (1940)

1 *Dead Men Tell* (1941)

1 *Charlie Chan in Rio* (1941)

1 *Castle in the Desert* (1942)

1 *Charlie Chan in the Secret Service* (1944)

1 *The Chinese Cat* (1944)

1 *Black Magic* (1944)

1 *The Jade Mask* (1945)

1 *The Scarlet Clue* (1945)

1 *The Shanghai Cobra* (1945)

1 *The Red Dragon* (1945)

1 *Dark Alibi* (1946)

1 *Shadows Over Chinatown* (1946)

1 *Dangerous Money* (1946)

1 *The Trap* (1947)

Charlie Chan in Honolulu (1938)

Sidney Toler . . . . Charlie Chan
Phyllis Brooks . . . . Judy Hayes
Sen Yung . . . . James Chan
Eddie Collins . . . . Al Hogan
John King . . . . George Randolph
Claire Dodd . . . . Mrs. Carol Wayne,
alias for Mrs. Elsie Hillman
George Zucco . . . . Dr. Cardigan
Robert Barrat . . . . Captain Johnson
Marc Lawrence. . . . . Johnny McCoy
Richard Lane . . . . . Detective Joe Arnold, alias for Mike Hannigan
Layne Tom, Jr. . . . . Tommy Chan
Philip Ahn . . . . Wing Foo
Paul Harvey . . . . Inspector Rawlins

- *As ancient ancestor once say, "As mind is fed with silent thought, so should body absorb its food." (Chan family)*

- *Bills sometimes more difficult to collect than murder clues. (Jimmy Chan)*

- *Hospitals for the sick—not playgrounds for healthy. (Chan family)*

- *When money talks, few are deaf. (Capt. Johnson and Jimmy Chan)*

- *Opinion like tea leaf in hot water—both need time for brewing. (Detective Arnold)*

- *Making bedfellow of serpent no guarantee against snake bite. (Detective Arnold)*

- *Caution very good life insurance. (Jimmy Chan)*

- *Bait only good if fish bite on same. (Jimmy Chan)*

Charlie Chan in Reno (1939)

Sidney Toler . . . . Charlie Chan
Ricardo Cortez . . . . Dr. Ainsley
Phyllis Brooks . . . . Vivian Wells
Slim Summerville . . . . . . Sheriff Tombstone Fletcher
Kane Richmond . . . . Curtis Whitman
Sen Yung . . . . James Chan
Pauline Moore . . . . Mary Whitman
Eddie Collins . . . . Cab driver
Kay Linaker . . . . Mrs. Russell
Louise Henry . . . . Jeanne Bently
Robert Lowery . . . . Wally Burke
Charles D. Brown . . . . Chief of Police King
Iris Wong . . . . Choy Wong
Morgan Conway . . . . George Bently
Hamilton MacFadden . . . . Night clerk

- *Man yet to be born who can tell what woman will or will not do. (Curtis Whitman)*

- *Very difficult to believe ill of those we love. (Curtis Whitman)*

- *Ancient ancestor once say, "Words cannot cook rice." (Curtis Whitman)*

- *Tombstones often engraved with words of wisdom. (Sheriff Fletcher)*

- *Charming company turn lowly sandwich into rich banquet. (Vivian Wells)*

- *If want wild bird to sing–do not put him in cage. (Sheriff Fletcher)*

- *When searching for needle in haystack, haystack only sensible location. (Mrs. Russell)*

- *Sometimes must strike innocent to trap guilty. (Sheriff Fletcher)*

- *Praise in any language very sweet. (Choy Wong)*

- *Sometimes tears from woman very happy sign. (Mary Whitman)*

Charlie Chan at Treasure Island (1939)

Sidney Toler	Charlie Chan
Cesar Romero	Fred Rhadini
Pauline Moore	Eve Cairo
Sen Yung	Jimmy Chan
Douglas Fowley	Pete Lewis
June Gale	Myra Rhadini
Douglass Dumbrille	Thomas Gregory, alias for Stewart Salisbury
Sally Blane	Stella Essex
Billie Seward	Bessie Sibley
Wally Vernon	Elmer Kelner
Donald MacBride	Chief J.J. Kilvaine
Charles Halton	Redley
Trevor Bardette	Abdul
Louis Jean Heydt	Paul Essex

- *One scholar in family better than two detectives. (Jimmy Chan)*

- *Unhappy news sometimes correct self next day. (Paul Essex)*

- *Impossible to miss someone who will always be in heart. (Stella Essex)*

- *Sometimes black magic very close relative to blackmail. (Chief Kilvaine, Pete Lewis and Fred Rhadini)*

- *Do not challenge supernatural unless armed with sword of truth. (Jimmy Chan)*

- *Advise caution, even draperies may have ears. (Pete Lewis and Fred Rhadini)*

- *If request music, must be willing to pay for fiddler. (Pete Lewis and Fred Rhadini)*

- *To destroy false prophet, must first unmask him before eyes of believers. (Pete Lewis and Fred Rhadini)*

- *Father who depend on son is happy or foolish according to son. (Jimmy Chan)*

- *Little mouse lucky his clothes do not fit elephant. (Jimmy Chan)*

- *Finger of death fits glove perfectly. (Abdul the Turk)*

- *Favorite pastime of man is fooling himself. (Pete Lewis)*

- *If befriend donkey, expect to be kicked. (Jimmy Chan)*

- *Swelled head sometimes give police more cooperation than criminal mistake. (Jimmy Chan and Pete Lewis)*

- *Obvious clues, like tricks in magic usually prove deceptive. (Jimmy Chan)*

City in Darkness (1939)

Sidney Toler . . . . Charlie Chan
Lynn Bari. . . . . Marie Dubon
Richard Clarke . . . . Tony Madero
Harold Huber . . . . Marcel
Pedro de Córdoba . . . . Antoine
Dorothy Tree . . . . Charlotte Ronnell
C. Henry Gordon . . . . . . Romaine, Prefect of police
Douglass Dumbrille . . . . Petroff
Noel Madison . . . . Beleseu
Leo Carroll . . . . Louis Santelle
Lon Chaney, Jr. . . . . Pierre
Louis Mercier. . . . . "Gentleman" Max
George Davis . . . . Alex
Barbara Leonard . . . . Lola
Adrienne d'Ambricourt . . . . Landlady
Frederick Vogeding . . . . Captain

- *Have not prepared for emergency—like man who buy suit with only one pair of pants. (Marcel)*

- *First war profiteer like early bird—look for big fat worm. (Santelle and Romaine)*

- *Birds never divide worm until safe in nest. (Marcel)*

- *In every city there are roosts where birds of feather congregate. (Marcel)*

- *Patience big sister to wisdom. (Marcel)*

- *Quite evident sugar daddy attract many butterflies. (Marcel)*

- *Confucius said, "A wise man questions himself—a fool, others." (Santelle and Pierre)*

- *Acid very poor oil to loosen stubborn tongue. (Santelle)*
- *Truth is only path out of tangled web. (Marie Dubon)*
- *To describe bitter medicine will not improve its flavor. (Marcel)*
- *Very difficult to drive car forward while looking backward. (Marcel)*
- *Wise man has said, "Beware of spider who invite fly into parlor." (Romaine and Antoine)*

Charlie Chan in Panama (1940)

Sidney Toler . . . . Charlie Chan, alias Fu Yuen
Jean Rogers . . . . Kathi Lenesch, also as Baroness
Kathi von Czardas
Lionel Atwill . . . . Cliveden Compton
Mary Nash . . . . Miss Jennie Finch, alias for Reiner
Sen Yung . . . . Jimmy Chan
Kane Richmond . . . . Richard Cabot
Chris-Pin Martin . . . . Lt. Montero
Lionel Royce . . . . Dr. Rudolph Grosser
Helen Ericson . . . . Stewardess
Jack La Rue . . . . Emil Manolo
Edwin Stanley . . . . . . Governor Col. D.C. Webster
Donald Douglas . . . . Capt. Lewis
Frank Puglia . . . . Achmed Halide
Addison Richards . . . . R.J. Godley
Edward Keane . . . . Dr. Fredericks

- *Thousand friends too few, one enemy too many. (R.J. Godley)*

- *Man without relatives is man without troubles. (Jimmy Chan)*

- *When prepared for worst, can hope for best. (Jimmy Chan)*

- *Young brain like grass need dew of sleep. (Jimmy Chan)*

- *Truth win more friendship than lies. (Kathi Lenesch)*

- *On soil of democracy you are safe from persecution. (Kathi Lenesch)*

- *Bad alibi like dead fish—cannot stand test of time. (Jimmy Chan)*

- *No heart strong enough to hold bullet. (Jimmy Chan)*
- *Features familiar as markings on bad penny. (Jennie Finch)*
- *Nerves make time crawl backward. (Jennie Finch)*
- *Dividing line between folly and wisdom very faint. (Jennie Finch)*
- *Patience leads to knowledge. (Kathi Lenesch and Richard Cabot)*

Charlie Chan's Murder Cruise (1940)

Sidney Toler . . . . Charlie Chan
Marjorie Weaver. . . . . Paula Drake
Lionel Atwill . . . . Dr. Suderman
Sen Yung . . . . Jimmy Chan
Robert Lowery . . . . Dick Kenyon
Don Beddoe . . . . James Ross
Leo Carroll. . . . . . Professor Gordon, alias for Jim Eberhardt
Cora Witherspoon. . . . . Susie Watson
Kay Linaker . . . . Mrs. Pendleton
Harlan Briggs . . . . Coroner
Charles Middleton . . . . Mr. Jeremiah Walters
Claire DuBrey . . . . Mrs. Sarah Walters
Leonard Mudie . . . . Gerald Pendleton
James Burke . . . . Wilkie
Richard Keene. . . . . Buttons
Layne Tom, Jr.. . . . . Willie Chan
Montague Shaw . . . . Inspector Duff

- *Like cotton wool—filial devotion softens weight of parental crown. (Jimmy Chan and Willie Chan)*

- *Sometimes quickest way to brain of young sprout is by impression on other end. (Inspector Duff)*

- *Better ten times a victim, than let one man go hungry. (Professor Gordon and beggar)*

- *Truth like oil—will in time rise to surface. (Dr. Suderman)*

- *To speak without thinking is to shoot without aiming. (Jimmy Chan)*

- *Life has been risked for jewels far less valuable than friendship. (Dr. Suderman and Professor Gordon)*

- *Hours are happiest when hands are busiest. (Jimmy Chan)*

- *Man can more safely search for gold if world thinks he dig ditch. (Jimmy Chan)*

- *In China mahjongg very simple; in America very complex—like modern life. (Professor Gordon and Dick Kenyon)*

- *When Chinese emperor have eight suspects of murder, he solve problem very quickly—chop off eight heads—always sure of getting one criminal...Not always easy to reduce many suspects to one. (Professor Gordon and Dick Kenyon)*

- *Elusive offspring like privacy—sometimes hard to find. (Jeremiah Walters)*

- *Judge always honorable position. (Jimmy Chan)*

- *Young man's explanation like skin of sensitive woman—very thin. (Paula Drake)*

- *One cloud does not make storm, nor one falsehood criminal. (Paula Drake)*

- *Dead men need no protection. (Dr. Suderman)*

- *Better a father lose his son than a detective his memory. (Jimmy Chan)*

- *In darkness, sometimes difficult to distinguish hawk from vulture. (Jimmy Chan)*

- *Memory of Number Two son still elusive—like soap in bathtub. (Jimmy Chan)*

- *After wedding bells prefer no phone bells. (Paula Drake and Dick Kenyon)*

Charlie Chan at the Wax Museum (1940)

Sidney Toler . . . . Charlie Chan
Sen Yung . . . . Jimmy Chan
C. Henry Gordon . . . . Dr. Cream
Marc Lawrence . . . . Steve McBirney
Joan Valerie . . . . Lily Latimer
Marguerite Chapman . . . . Mary Bolton
Ted Osborn . . . . Tom Agnew, alias for Butcher Degan
Michael Visaroff . . . . Dr. Otto von Brom
Hilda Vaughn . . . . Mrs. Rocke
Charles Wagenheim . . . . Willie Fern
Archie Twitchell . . . . Carter Lane
Edward Marr . . . . Grennock
Joe King . . . . Inspector O'Matthews
Harold Goodwin . . . . Edwards

- *Always prefer to utilize element of surprise—never to be victim. (Inspector O'Matthews)*

- *Only very foolish mouse make nest in cat's ear. (Inspector O'Matthews)*

- *Any powder that kills flea is good powder. (Jimmy Chan)*

- *Will imitate woman and change mind. (Dr. Cream)*

- *Knowledge only gained through curiosity. (Inspector O'Matthews)*

- *Mice only play when cat supposed to be in bed. (Inspector O'Matthews)*

- *Old solution sometimes like ancient egg. (Dr. Otto Von Brom)*

- *Justice can be brought to dead man. (Tom Agnew)*

- *Truth speak from any chair. (Lily Latimer)*

- *Every bird seek its own tree—never tree the bird. (Dr. Otto Von Brom)*

- *Suspicion is only toy of fools. (Jimmy Chan)*

- *Filial grief honorable music to ancient heart. (Jimmy Chan)*

- *Fingerprints may have message. (Jimmy Chan)*

- *Sometimes better to see and not tell. (Jimmy Chan)*

- *Fear is cruel padlock. (Inspector O'Matthews)*

- *Mock insanity not always safe alibi. (Mrs. Joe Rocke)*

- *Justice like virtue—brings its own reward. (Mrs. Joe Rocke)*

Murder Over New York (1940)

Sidney Toler	Charlie Chan
Marjorie Weaver	Patricia West
Robert Lowery	David Elliot
Ricardo Cortez	George Kirby
Donald MacBride	Inspector Vance
Melville Cooper	Herbert Fenton
Joan Valerie	June Preston
Kane Richmond	Ralph Percy
Sen Yung	Jimmy Chan
John Sutton	Keith Jeffrey, alias for Paul Narvo
Leyland Hodgson	Boggs
Clarence Muse	Butler
Frederick Worlock	Hugh Drake
Lal Chand Mehra	Ramullah

- *Officer of law cannot escape long arm of same. (Inspector Hugh Drake)*

- *Needle can be found when correct thread located. (Inspector Hugh Drake)*

- *British tenacity with Chinese patience like royal flush in poker game—unbeatable. (Inspector Hugh Drake)*

- *Canary, unlike unfaithful dog, do not die for sympathy. (Jimmy Chan and George Kirby)*

- *Coincidence like ancient egg—leave unpleasant odor. (Jimmy Chan)*

- *Thought at present like dog chasing own tail—getting no place. (Jimmy Chan)*

- *Nut easy to crack often empty. (Jimmy Chan)*

- *Will inform honorable mother that aid from Number two*

son like interest on mortgage, impossible to escape. (Jimmy Chan)

- *Fresh weed better than wilted rose. (Jimmy Chan)*
- *Person who ask riddle should know answer. (June Preston)*
- *Happy solution never see light if truth kept in dark. (Patricia West)*
- *One man with gun have more authority than whole army with no ammunition. (Jimmy Chan)*
- *Door of opportunity swing both ways. (Jimmy Chan)*
- *Wishful thinking sometimes lead to blind alley. (Inspector Vance)*
- *Faces may alter, but fingerprints never lie. (Inspector Vance)*
- *Important events, like insistent alarm clock, demand attention. (Herbert Fenton)*
- *Eye easily deceived. (Patricia West)*
- *Same leopard can hide under different spots. (Patricia West)*
- *Kitchen stove most excellent weapon—good for cooking goose. (Herbert Fenton)*
- *Desire to live still strongest instinct in man. (David Elliot)*
- *Confidence of favorite son like courage of small boy at dentist—most evident after tooth extracted. (Inspector Vance)*

Dead Men Tell (1941)

Sidney Toler	Charlie Chan
Sheila Ryan	Kate Ransome
Robert Weldon	Steve Daniels
Sen Yung	Jimmy Chan
Don Douglas	Jed Thomasson
Katharine Aldridge	Laura Thursday
Paul McGrath	Charles Thursday
George Reeves	Bill Lydig
Truman Bradley	Captain Kane
Ethel Griffies	Miss Patience Nodbury
Lenita Lane	Dr. Anne Bonney
Milton Parsons	Gene LaFarge

- *Desire for ocean adventure is ailment very much like hives—give itch to many boys. (Patience Nodbury)*

- *Man has learned much who has learned how to die. (Patience Nodbury)*

- *Message sometimes hide in magic of practical joke. (Steve Daniels and Jed Thomasson)*

- *Swallow much but digest little. (Jimmy Chan)*

- *Trouble like first love—teach many lessons. (Jimmy Chan and Dr. Bonney)*

Charlie Chan in Rio (1941)

Sidney Toler . . . . Charlie Chan
Mary Beth Hughes . . . . Joan Reynolds
Cobina Wright, Jr. . . . . Grace Ellis
Ted North. . . . . Clark Denton
Victor Jory . . . . . Alfredo Marana, alias for Alfredo Cardozo
Harold Huber . . . . Chief Inspector Souto
Sen Yung . . . . Jimmy Chan
Richard Derr . . . . Ken Reynolds
Jacqueline Dalya . . . . . Lola Dean, alias for Lola Wagner
Kay Linaker . . . . . . Helen Ashby, alias for Barbara Cardozo
Truman Bradley. . . . . Paul Wagner
Hamilton MacFadden . . . . Bill Kellogg
Leslie Dennison . . . . Rice
Iris Wong. . . . . Lili Wong
Eugene Borden . . . . Armando
Ann Codee . . . . Margo

- *Interesting problem in chemistry— sweet wine often turn nice woman sour. (Chief Souto)*

- *Biggest mistakes in history made by people who didn't think. (Chief Souto and Jimmy Chan)*

- *Pretty girl like lap dog—sometimes go mad. (Jimmy Chan)*

- *Long experience teach until murderer found, suspect everybody. (Chief Souto)*

- *Good policy to have murderer consider detective dope. (Jimmy, as translated from Chinese)*

- *Slippery man sometimes slip in own oil. (Jimmy Chan)*

- *Experience teach, unless eyewitness present, every murder case is long shot. (Chief Souto)*

- *Prefer not to walk across before coming to bridge. (Bill Kellogg)*

- *To one who kill, life can suddenly become most precious. (Helen Ashby)*

- *Fruits of labor sometimes very bitter. (Chief Souto)*

Castle in the Desert (1942)

Sidney Toler . . . . Charlie Chan
Arleen Whelan . . . . Brenda Hartford
Richard Derr. . . . . Carl Detheridge
Douglass Dumbrille . . . . Paul Manderley
Henry Daniell . . . . . . Watson King, alias for Cesare Borgia
Edmund MacDonald . . . . Walter Hartford
Sen Yung . . . . Jimmy Chan
Lenita Lane. . . . . . Lucy Manderley, formerly known as Princess
. . . . Lucrezia della Borgia
Ethel Griffies . . . . Madame Lily Saturnia
Milton Parsons. . . . . Arthur Fletcher
Steve Geray . . . . Dr. Retling
Lucien Littlefield . . . . Professor Gleason

- *Man who walk have both feet on ground. (Jimmy Chan)*

- *Guardhouse excellent guarantee for offspring. (Jimmy Chan)*

- *Man without enemies like dog without fleas. (Madam Lily Saturnia)*

- *Desert without Indians very safe. (Madam Lily Saturnia)*

- *Man who fear death die thousand times. (Madam Lily Saturnia)*

- *To study Eskimo or African pigmy, anthropologist must make their home his home. (Paul Manderley)*

- *Caution sometimes mother of suspicion. (Dr. Retling)*

- *Practical joke sometimes disguise for sinister motive. (Lucy Manderley)*

- *Lovers use element of surprise—also criminals. (Lucy Manderley)*

- *Guilty conscience like dog in circus—many tricks. (Paul Manderley)*

- *Man cannot avoid destiny. (Madam Lily Saturnia)*

- *Sometimes solution to murder problem does not require scandal. (Dr. Retling)*

- *Glamour boy who jump to conclusion sometimes get hair mussed. (Jimmy Chan)*

- *Theory like thunderstorm—very wet. (Jimmy Chan)*

- *Sharp wit sometimes better than deadly weapon. (Watson King)*

- *Timid man never win lottery prize. (Paul Manderley)*

- *Elaborate excuse seldom truth. (Paul Manderley)*

Charlie Chan in the Secret Service (1944)

Sidney Toler . . . . Charlie Chan
Mantan Moreland . . . . Birmingham Brown
Arthur Loft . . . . Jones
Gwen Kenyon . . . . Inez Arranto
Sarah Edwards . . . . Mrs. Hargue
George Lewis . . . . Paul Arranto
Marianne Quon . . . . Iris Chan
Benson Fong . . . . Tommy Chan
Muni Seroff . . . . Peter Laska
Barry Bernard . . . . David Blake
Gene Stutenroth . . . . Luiz Philipe Vega,
alias for Philipe von Vegan
Eddie Chandler . . . . Lewis
Lelah Tyler . . . . . . Mrs. Winters, alias for Fraulein Manleck

- *When alibi pushed at me—always suspect motive in woodpile. (Luiz Vega)*

- *Detective without curiosity is like glass eye at keyhole—no good. (Luiz Vega)*

- *Children go through life with same tact as tornado. (All assembled suspects)*

- *Murderer always choose weapon he know best. (Luiz Vega)*

- *If man place himself in way of finger of suspicion, must not be surprised if he receive poke in the eye. (Paul Arranto)*

- *Suspicion like rain—fall on just and unjust. (Paul Arranto)*

- *You are like business end of water spout—always running off at mouth (Tommy Chan)*

The Chinese Cat (1944)

Sidney Toler . . . . Charlie Chan
Joan Woodbury . . . . Leah Manning
Mantan Moreland . . . . Birmingham Brown
Benson Fong . . . . Tommy Chan
Ian Keith . . . . Dr. Paul Rednick
Cy Kendall . . . . Webster Deacon
Weldon Heyburn . . . . Detective Harvey Dennis
Anthony Warde . . . . Catlen
John Davidson . . . . Carl Karzoff/Kurt Karzoff
Dewey Robinson. . . . . Salos
Stan Jolley . . . . Gannett
Betty Blythe . . . . Mrs. Manning
Jack Norton . . . . Hotel desk clerk
Luke Chan . . . . Wu Song

- *Any detective will tell you all mystery novels most horrible. (Leah Manning)*

- *Authors sometimes take strange liberties. (Leah Manning)*

- *Your assistance about as welcomed as water in a leaking ship. (Tommy Chan)*

- *You talk like rooster who think sun come up just to hear him crow. (Tommy Chan)*

- *Expert is merely man who make quick decisions—and is sometimes right. (Dr. Paul Rednick)*

- *Fear you are weak limb to which no family tree may point with pride. (Tommy Chan)*

- *Fear of future is wrong for young people in love. You should get married and raise large family. Once you have large family, all other troubles mean nothing. (Sgt. Harvey Dennis and Leah Manning)*

- *Never start anything until I see end of road. (Dr. Paul Rednick)*

- *Dog cannot chase three rabbits at the same time. (Tommy Chan and Birmingham Brown)*

- *Manning case like modern highway—sooner or later come to detour. (Tommy Chan and Birmingham Brown)*

- *Manning case like puzzle—wrong pieces appear. (Tommy Chan)*

- *You are like turtle. After everything all over, you stick head out and find truth right under your very nose. (Tommy Chan)*

Black Magic, aka *Murder at Midnight* (1944)

Sidney Toler	as Charlie Chan
Mantan Moreland	Birmingham Brown
Frances Chan	Frances Chan
Joseph Crehan	Inspector Matthews
Helen Beverley	Norma Duncan, alias Nancy Woods
Jacqueline deWitt	Justine Bonner
Geraldine Wall	Harriet Green
Ralph Peters	Officer Rafferty
Frank Jaquet	Paul Hamlin, a.k.a. Chardo
Edward Earle	Dawson
Claudia Dell	Vera Starkey
Harry Depp	Charles Edwards
Charles Jordan	Tom Starkey
Dick Gordon	William Bonner

- *Shady business do not make for sunny life. (Justine Bonner)*
- *Spirits always have a long way to come. (Harriet Green)*

The Jade Mask (1945)

Sidney Toler . . . . Charlie Chan
Mantan Moreland . . . . Birmingham Brown
Edwin Luke . . . . Eddie Chan
Hardie Albright . . . . Walter Meeker
Frank Reicher . . . . Mr. Harper
Janet Warren . . . . Jean Kent
Cyril Delevanti . . . . Roth
Alan Bridge. . . . . Sheriff Mack
Ralph Lewis . . . . Officer Jim Kimball
Dorothy Granger . . . . Stella Graham
Edith Evanson . . . . Louise Harper
Joe Whitehead . . . . Dr. Samuel R. Peabody
Henry Hall . . . . Inspector Godfrey
Jack Ingram . . . . Lloyd Archer,
also disguised as Walter Meeker
Danny Desmond . . . . Bellboy

- *No barber shave so close but another barber find some work to do. (Sheriff Mack and Officer Godfrey)*

- *Every time you open your mouth you put in more feet than centipede. (Edward Chan)*

- *To get information from him is like putting empty bucket into empty well. (Sheriff Mack)*

- *Things misplaced sometimes furnish very good clues. (Sheriff Mack and Louise Harper)*

- *Murder know no law of relativity. (Sheriff Mack)*

- *My boy, if silence is golden, you are bankrupt. (Edward Chan)*

- *Like fingerprints, no human ears are exactly alike. (Stella Graham)*

The Scarlet Clue (1945)

Sidney Toler . . . . Charlie Chan
Mantan Moreland . . . . Birmingham Brown
Ben Carter . . . . as himself
Benson Fong . . . . Tommy Chan
Virginia Brissac . . . . Mrs. Marsh
Robert E. Homans . . . . Capt. Flynn
Jack Norton . . . . Willie Rand
Janet Shaw . . . . Gloria Bayne
Helen Devereaux . . . . Diane Hall
Victoria Faust . . . . Hulda Swenson

- *Contents of safe only secure so long as someone outside watching same. (Mr. Hamilton)*
- *What detective needs is great patience. (Tommy Chan)*
- *So many fish in fish market—even flower smell same. (Capt. Flynn)*

The Shanghai Cobra (1945)

Sidney Toler . . . . Charlie Chan
Mantan Moreland . . . . Birmingham Brown
Benson Fong . . . . Tommy Chan
James Cardwell . . . . Ned Stewart
Joan Barclay . . . . . . Paula Webb, alias Pauline Webster
Addison Richards . . . . . Jan Van Horn, alias John Adams
Arthur Loft . . . . . Bradford Harris, alias Special Agent Hume
Janet Warren . . . . Lorraine
Gene Stutenroth . . . . Morgan
Joe Devlin . . . . Taylor
James Flavin . . . . H.R. Jarvis
Roy Gordon . . . . Walter Fletcher
Walter Fenner . . . . Inspector Harry Davis

- *In my business always expect to find something wrong. (Walter Fletcher)*

- *Ancient ancestor once say, "Even wise man cannot fathom depth of woman's smile." (Ned Stewart)*

- *Cannot sell bear skin before shooting bear. (Tommy Chan)*

- *Police do not read Emily Post. (Walter Fletcher)*

- *Mice will never play so long as cat is in house. (Inspector Harry Davis)*

- *Too many hands sometimes spoil pudding. (Ned Stewart)*

The Red Dragon (1945)

Sidney Toler	Charlie Chan
Fortunio Bonanova.	Inspector Luis Carvero
Benson Fong	Tommy Chan
Robert E. Keane.	Alfred Wyans
Willie Best.	Chattanooga Brown
Carol Hughes.	Marguerite Fontan
Marjorie Hoshelle	Countess Irena
Barton Yarborough	Joseph Bradish
George Meeker	Edmund Slade
Don Costello.	Charles Masack
Charles Trowbridge	Prentiss
Mildred Boyd.	Josephine
Jean Wong	Iris Ling
Donald Dexter Taylor	Walter Dorn

- *Assistants should be seen and not heard. (Tommy Chan and Chattanooga Brown)*

- *Puppy cannot fool old dog. (Tommy Chan)*

- *Good detective always look for something unusual. (Luis Carvero and Tommy Chan)*

- *Hens sit often, but they lay eggs. (Tommy Chan and Chattanooga Brown)*

- *Will repeat old police slogan, "Unusual thing always very good clue." (Luis Carvero)*

- *Like Chinese army, Chinese ink cannot be wiped out. (Luis Carvero)*

- *Number Three son is like rooster who thinks sun come up just to hear him crow. (Tommy Chan)*

Dark Alibi (1946)

Sidney Toles . . . . Charlie Chan
Mantan Moreland . . . . Birmingham Brown
Ben Carter . . . . Ben Carter
Benson Fong . . . . Tommy Chan
Teala Loring . . . . June Harley
George Holmes . . . . Hugh Kenzie
Joyce Compton . . . . Emily Evans
John Eldredge . . . . Anthony R. Morgan
Russell Hicks . . . . Warden Cameron
Tim Ryan . . . . Foggy
Janet Shaw . . . . Miss Petrie
Edward Earle . . . . Thomas Harley
Ray Walker . . . . Mr. Danvers
Milton Parsons . . . . Mr. Johnson
Edna Holland . . . . Mrs. Foss
Anthony Warde . . . . Jimmy Slade
George Eldredge . . . . Brand
Meyer Grace . . . . Doorman

- *Ancient proverb say, "One small wind can raise much dust." (Anthony Morgan and June Harley)*

- *Wish you would wear out brains instead of seat of pants. (Tommy Chan and Birmingham)*

- *Honorable grandmother once say, "Do not think of future—it come too soon." (June Harley and Hugh Kenzie)*

- *He is like tooth which has been pulled—tooth is missing but gap remains. From gap we may deduce why tooth is gone. (June Harley and Hugh Kenzie)*

- *Ugliest trade sometimes have moment of joy. Even gravedigger know some people for whom he would do his work with extreme pleasure. (Mrs. Foss)*

- *Remember old saying, "Earthquake may shatter the rock but sand upon which rock stood still right there in same old place." (June Harley and Hugh Kenzie)*

- *Never believe nightmare no matter how real it may seem. (Thomas Harley)*

- *Skeleton in closets speak loudest to police. (Anthony Morgan)*

- *No experiment failure until last experiment is success. (Anthony Morgan and Mr. Thompson)*

Shadows Over Chinatown (1946)

Sidney Toler . . . . Charlie Chan
Mantan Moreland . . . . Birmingham Brown
Victor Sen Young . . . . Jimmy Chan
Tanis Chandler . . . . . . Mary Conover, alias Mary McCoy
John Gallaudet . . . . . . Jeff Hay, alias for Craig Winfield
Paul Bryar . . . . Mike Rogan
Bruce Kellogg . . . . Joe Thompson, alias Jack Tilford
Alan Bridge . . . . Capt. Allen
Mary Gordon . . . . Mrs. Conover
Dorothy Granger . . . . Joan Mercer
Jack Norton . . . . Cosgrove
George Eldredge . . . . Chief Brannigan
Tyra Vaughn . . . . Miss Chalmers
Lyle Latell . . . . Police clerk
Myra McKinney . . . . Kate Johnson
Gladys Blake . . . . Myrtle

- *Numbers cannot control life expectancy. (Birmingham Brown)*

- *Goods returned, crime prevented. (Mr. Gosgrove)*

- *As nurse say to father of newborn twins—pleasure is double. (Chief Brannigan)*

- *Sometime surgeon's scar speak louder than fingerprints. (Capt. Allen)*

- *Confucius say, "Sleep only escape from yesterday." (Mrs. Conover)*

- *Business conversation at table very bad for digestion. (Tommy Chan)*

- *Number Two son like flea on dog—must have fine-toothed comb to find same. (Birmingham Brown)*

- *Deception is bad game for amateurs. (Joseph Thompson)*

- *Ancient proverb say, "Never bait trap with wolf to catch wolf." (Mary Conover and Joseph Thompson)*

- *Cornered rat full of fight. (Police car driver)*

Dangerous Money (1946)

Sidney Toler . . . . Charlie Chan
Gloria Warren. . . . . Rona Simmonds
Victor Sen Young . . . . Jimmy Chan
Rick Vallin . . . . Tao Erickson
Joseph Crehan . . . . Captain Black
Willie Best. . . . . Chattanooga Brown
John Harmon . . . . Freddie Kirk
Bruce Edwards. . . . . Harold Mayfair
Dick Elliott . . . . P.T. Burke
Joe Allen, Jr. . . . . George Brace
Amira Moustafa . . . . Laura Erickson
Tristram Coffin . . . . Scott Pearson
Alan Douglas . . . . . Mrs. Whipple, alias for Joseph Murdock
Selmer Jackson . . . . Ship's doctor
Dudley Dickerson . . . . Big Ben
Rito Punay . . . . Pete
Elaine Lange . . . . Cynthia Martin
Emmett Vogan . . . . Professor Dick Martin
Leslie Dennison . . . . Reverend Whipple, alias
for Theodore M. Lane

- *Problem rarely wait for clearing weather. (Scott Pearson)*

- *There is old saying, "Good wife's place should be at mate's elbow in time of trouble." (Tao and Laura Erickson)*

- *Tiger going away from village is never feared. (Capt. Black)*

- *Guilty mind sometimes pinch worse than ancient boot of torture. (George Brace and Rona Simmonds)*

- *Hasty man could also drink tea with fork. (Jimmy Chan and Chattanooga Brown)*

- *Each country's dance is most beautiful in that particular country. (Laura Erickson)*

- *Kangaroo reaches destination also by leaps and bounds. (Capt. Black)*

- *Good hunter never break twig under foot. (Capt. Black)*

The Trap (1947)

Sidney Toler . . . . Charlie Chan
Mantan Moreland . . . . Birmingham Brown
Victor Sen Young . . . . Jimmy Chan
Tanis Chandler . . . . Adelaide
Larry Blake . . . . Rick Daniels
Kirk Alyn . . . . Sergeant Reynolds
Rita Quigley . . . . Clementine
Anne Nagel . . . . Marcia
Helen Gerald . . . . Ruby
Howard Negley . . . . Cole King
Lois Austin . . . . Mrs. Thorn
Barbara Jean Wong . . . . San Toy
Minerva Urecal . . . . Mrs. Weebles
Margaret Brayton . . . . Madge Mudge
Bettie Best . . . . Winifred
Jane Bryant . . . . Lois

- *Mistake sometimes bring most fortunate relief. (Mrs. Thorn)*

- *Obstructing justice is a very serious crime. (Rick Daniels)*

- *Best laid plans of mice and men go a little bit haywire. (Doc Brandt and Adelaide)*

- *Puzzle always deepest near the center. (Doc Brandt and Adelaide)*

- *Leisurely hunter have time to stalk prey, but hunter in haste must set trap. (Jimmy Chan and San Toy)*

Roland Winters as Charlie Chan

With Winter's role, Charlie Chan is portrayed as a private detective living in San Francisco with no mention of his wife or family. Unlike Warner Oland and Sidney Toler, Winters' prominent nose and blond hair would have never allowed him to pass for an Oriental without some adjustments. Winters would squint to give his eyes a slanted appearance and to reduce the prominence of his nose. Winters always looked straight into the camera and if he were talking to someone to his side, he would merely move his eyes right or left.

While Winters' six low-budget entries are generally disliked by *Charlie Chan* movie buffs, it can now be seen that Winters brought a much needed breath of fresh air to the flagging film series with his self-mocking, semi-satirical interpretation of Charlie, which is very close to the Charlie Chan in Biggers' novels.

Roland Winters (1947–1949)

Charlie Chan Filmography
Roland Winters

- *The Chinese Ring* (1947)
- *Docks of New Orleans* (1948)
- *The Shanghai Chest* (1948)
- *The Golden Eye* (1948)
- *The Feathered Serpent* (1948)
- *The Sky Dragon* (1949)

The Chinese Ring (1947)

Roland Winters . . . . Charlie Chan
Warren Douglas . . . . Sergeant Bill Davidson
Mantan Moreland . . . . Birmingham Brown
Louise Currie . . . . Peggy Cartwright
Victor Sen Young. . . . . Tommy Chan
Philip Ahn . . . . Captain Kong
Byron Foulger . . . . Mr. Armstrong
Thayer Roberts. . . . . Captain James J. Kelso
Jean Wong . . . . Princess Mei Ling
Chabing . . . . Lilly Mae Wong
George L. Spaulding . . . . Dr. Hickey

- *Death my son is the reckoning of heaven—in this case, most complicated reckoning. (Tommy Chan)*

- *Strange events permit themselves the luxury of occurring in strange places. (Sgt. Davidson)*

- *Old father once say, "Politeness golden key to many doors." (Sgt. Davidson)*

- *Many questions arise—all, in good time, we get answers. (Sgt. Davidson)*

- *Sometimes think successful detective one upon whom luck shows smiling countenance. (Mr. Armstrong)*

- *Man who ride on tiger cannot dismount. (Birmingham Brown)*

- *Confucius say, "Luck happy chain of foolish accident." (Sgt. Davidson)*

- *Woman not made for heavy thinking, but should always decorate scene like blossom of plumb. (Sgt. Davidson and Peggy Cartwright)*

- *Man who ride on merry-go-round all the time sooner or later must catch brass ring. (viewers at movie's end)*

Docks of New Orleans (1948)

Roland Winters . . . . Charlie Chan
Virginia Dale . . . . René
Mantan Moreland . . . . Birmingham Brown
John Gallaudet . . . . Capt. Pete McNalley
Victor Sen Young . . . . Tommy Chan
Carol Forman . . . . Nita Aguirre
Douglas Fowley . . . . Grock
Harry Hayden . . . . Dr. Oscar Swendstrom
Howard Negley. . . . . André Pereaux
Stanley Andrews. . . . . . . Theodore Von Scherbe
Emmett Vogan . . . . Henri Castanero
Boyd Irwin . . . . Simon Lafontaine
Rory Mallinson. . . . . Mr. Thompson
George J. Lewis. . . . . Sergeant Dansiger

- *He who takes whatever gods send with smile has learned life's hardest lesson. I personally find it difficult to achieve that smile. (Tommy Chan and Simon Lafontaine)*

- *Sometimes most essential clue very difficult to find. (Simon Lafontaine)*

- *If matter not solved, it is will of fate, but feel inclined to give fate small tussle. (Simon Lafontaine)*

- *Death one appointment we must all keep, and for which no time set. (Capt. McNalley)*

- *Looks sometimes are frightful liar. (Capt. McNalley)*

- *Patience. Must harvest rice before you can boil it. (Capt. McNalley)*

- *Even melon grown in shade will ripen in the end. (Tommy Chan and Capt. McNalley)*

- *The ignorant always loud in argument. (Tommy Chan)*
- *He who squanders today talking about yesterday's triumph have nothing to boast of tomorrow. (Pereaux)*
- *Must gather at leisure what may use in haste. (Nita Aguirre)*
- *It is fool in hurry who drink tea with fork. (Nita Aguirre)*
- *He who goes into hills after tiger must pay price. (Pereaux)*
- *Ship with too many pilots sometimes have difficulty reaching port. (Capt. McNalley)*
- *After dinner is over, who cares about spoon? (Birmingham Brown)*
- *Wherever one is not—that is where heart is. (Tommy Chan)*

The Shanghai Chest (1948)

Roland Winters . . . . Charlie Chan
Mantan Moreland . . . . Birmingham Brown
Tim Ryan . . . . Lt. Mike Ruark
Victor Sen Young . . . . Tommy Chan
Deannie Best . . . . Phyllis Powers
Tristram Coffin . . . . Ed Seward
John Alvin . . . . Victor Armstrong
Russell Hicks . . . . District Attorney Frank Bronson
Pierre Watkin . . . . Judge Wesley Armstrong
Philip Van Zandt . . . . Joseph Pindello
Milton Parsons . . . . Mr. Grail
Olaf Hytten . . . . Bates
Erville Alderson . . . . Walter Somerville
George Eldredge . . . . Pat Finley

- *Night in Bastille not exactly bed of roses. (Tommy Chan and Birmingham Brown)*

- *Happiest walk in life of mailman are on holiday. (Lt. Ruark)*

- *Sometimes better to lull suspected person with false sense of security. (Lt. Ruark)*

- *Surprised detective might as well clutch iron ball and dive in lake. (Lt. Ruark)*

- *Hardly worth exhibiting puzzle until more pieces fit together. Much must still be checked, but patience are virtue one must hug to bosom. (Lt. Ruark)*

- *Sometimes muddy waters, when stirred sufficiently, bring strange things to surface. (Lt. Ruark)*

- *Certain facts seem to gleam clear like snow on distant mountain top. (Phyllis Powers)*

- *So seldom brains and beauty dance in street together. (Phyllis Powers)*

- *Someone once say, "Out of mouths of babes come wisdom." (Tommy Chan)*

- *Man who have gun either afraid or have guilty conscience. (Mr. Grail)*

The Golden Eye (1948)

Roland Winters . . . . Charlie Chan
Wanda McKay . . . . Evelyn Manning
Mantan Moreland . . . . Birmingham Brown
Victor Sen Young . . . . Tommy Chan
Bruce Kellogg . . . . Talbot Bartlett
Tim Ryan . . . . Lt. Mike Ruark
Evelyn Brent . . . . Sister Teresa
Ralph Dunn . . . . Mr. Driscoll
Lois Austin . . . . Mrs. Margaret Driscoll
Forrest Taylor . . . . Manning
Lee "Lasses" White . . . . Pete

- *People who listen at keyhole rarely hear good of themselves. (Tommy Chan)*

- *Small things sometimes tell very large story. (Lt. Ruark)*

- *Desert present many mysteries. (Evelyn Manning and Talbot Bartlett)*

- *Small investigation sometimes bring large amount of knowledge. (Pete)*

- *Willingness to speak not necessarily mean willingness to act. (Birmingham Brown)*

- *Little knowledge sometimes very dangerous possession. (Tommy Chan)*

- *Bear should not toy with tiger. (Tommy Chan)*

The Feathered Serpent (1948)

Roland Winters . . . . Charlie Chan
Keye Luke . . . . Lee Chan
Mantan Moreland . . . . Birmingham Brown
Victor Sen Yung . . . . Tommy Chan
Carol Forman . . . . Sonia Cabot
Robert Livingston. . . . . John Stanley
Nils Asther . . . . Professor Paul Evans
Beverly Jons . . . . Joan Farnsworth
Martin Garralaga . . . . Pedro
George J. Lewis . . . . Capt. Juan Gonzalez
Leslie Dennison . . . . Professor Henry Farnsworth

- *Man who improve house before building solid foundation apt to run in very much trouble. (Tommy Chan)*

- *Sometimes human tissue tell more than human lips. (Professor John Stanley)*

- *Very difficult to estimate depth of well by size of bucket. (Professor Paul Evans)*

- *Guilty conscience always first to speak up. (Sonia Cabot)*

- *Hunch not sufficient evidence to convince jury of guilt. (Lee Chan)*

The Sky Dragon (1949)

Roland Winters . . . . Charlie Chan
Keye Luke . . . . Lee Chan
Mantan Moreland . . . . Birmingham Brown
Noel Neill . . . . Jane Marshall
Tim Ryan . . . . Lt. Mike Ruark
Iris Adrian . . . . Wanda LaFern
Elena Verdugo . . . . . . Connie Jackson, alias Marie Burke
Milburn Stone . . . . Tim Norton
Lyle Talbot . . . . Andy Barrett, alias Andrew J. Smith
Paul Maxey . . . . John Anderson
Joel Marston . . . . Don Blake
John Eldridge . . . . William E. French
Eddie Parks . . . . Jonathon Tibbetts
Louise Franklin . . . . Lena Franklin

- *Tired man's idea sometimes very much like child's nightmare—easily dispelled by bright light of day. (Lt. Ruark)*

- *Innocent act without thinking—guilty always make plans. (Lt. Ruark and Tim Norton)*

- *Revenge and profit two of oldest motives for murder and robbery. (Andy Barett)*

- *Justice must be blind to friendship. (Jane Marshall)*

- *Ideas planted too soon often like seeds on winter ground—quickly die. (Lt. Ruark)*

- *Case very much like photographic negative—proper development sometimes bring interesting things to light. (Wanda LaFern)*

- *To suspect is one thing—to have proof is another. (Lee Chan)*

- *Death, even to deserving, never pleasant. (Lt. Ruark and John Anderson)*

- *Wise playwright plan ahead so that movement of actors does not disturb play. (John Anderson)*

Miscellaneous Chan Quotes

The following aphorisms are those from *Quotations from Charlie Chan* that cannot be attributed to a specific film in the *Charlie Chan* series.

- *A fool and his money never become old acquaintances.*
- *A humble chariot, but always reliable, like model wife.*
- *A soft word does not scratch tongue.*
- *Always carry spare in case of blowout.*
- *Always danger where men are evil, but knowledge best weapon for protection.*
- *Always very hard winter when honorable cheese runs after mouse.*
- *Believe wise bird can tell much.*
- *Blind man feels ahead with cane before proceeding.*
- *Case still wide open, like swinging gate.*
- *Charm still best key to hospitality.*
- *Conscience rest heavy like sour rice in unworthy stomach.*
- *Crime never solved by books.*
- *Do not tangle foot in fringe of murder.*
- *Do not wave stick when trying to catch dog.*
- *Eager twig bend to duty.*
- *Empty as robin's nest in January.*
- *End of journey bring sadness.*
- *Events explode suddenly, like firecrackers in the face of innocent passerby.*
- *Every fence has two sides.*

- *Every day, when you are doing good deed, remember kind hearted elephant who tried to help hen hatch chicks. He sat down on little hen's eggs.*

- *Every man must wear out at least one pair of fool's shoes.*

- *Every Maybe has a wife called Maybe-Not.*

- *Evident bird of fine plumage escape sharp eye of eagle.*

- *Explain please, ability to stay with hunt without glimpse of fox.*

- *Fondly recall many chases, from cookie jar to back door.*

- *Friends, like fiddle strings, should not be stretched too tight.*

- *Good kitchens kill more men than sharp sword.*

- *Guest who linger too long—becomes stale like unused fish.*

- *Humbly suggest not to judge wine by barrel it is in.*

- *Innocent and guilty are harder to separate than Siamese twins.*

- *Inscrutable fates reveal step toward true solution.*

- *Intelligent defense of nation best guarantee for years of peace.*

- *Investigation best way to find answer.*

- *It takes two heads to make empty barrel.*

- *It takes very rainy day to drown duck.*

- *Law is honest man's eyeglass to see better.*

- *Like when eating peach—start outside and work to center.*

- *Luck, and help of inscrutable fates, extremely necessary.*

- *Man is not incurably drowned if he still knows he's all wet.*

- *Man who does not listen at keyhole never gets earache.*

- *Man who fights law always loses—same as grasshopper is always wrong in argument with chicken.*

- *Man who sits by side of road sees world pass by.*
- *Man's soul is lost that does not grieve at death of faithful servant.*
- *Maybe some people on sea of matrimony wish they had missed the boat.*
- *Mention of food more painful than surgeon's knife without anesthetic.*
- *Much fuel tempt man to build fire.*
- *Never hunt rabbit with dead dog.*
- *Nothing but the wind, can pass the sun without casting shadow.*
- *Old Chinese proverb say, "Where the mind is frightened, the tongue moves freely."*
- *On subject of drink, I am one-round prize fighter. Second round always knock-out.*
- *One at a time is good fishing.*
- *Only foolish mouse plays with cat.*
- *Only that man with ear to keyhole betray excessive curiosity.*
- *Opportunity knocks on door again.*
- *Out of the darkness of the unknown comes spark of light.*
- *Patience and mulberry leaf become a silk shawl.*
- *Politely suggest cooperation for good of all.*
- *Rain quenches unguarded fire.*
- *Regret such alibis have habit of disappearing like cheese in vicinity of mouse.*
- *Roundabout way often shortest path to correct destination.*
- *Silence is golden, except in police station.*
- *Sometimes beneath eyes that weep are teeth that laugh.*

- *Sometimes dull stone makes very sharp knife.*
- *Sometimes hope become scarce as midnight rainbow.*
- *Sometimes jewel found in ashes.*
- *Sometimes very small cloud hide sun.*
- *The goose who laid egg deserves the credit.*
- *The impossible sometimes permits itself the luxury of occurring.*
- *Time and analysis will tell.*
- *Time only wasted when sprinkling perfume on goat farm.*
- *To be found listening to what is not meant for your ears is to show that you have something to conceal.*
- *Too many mixed drinks make big headache.*
- *Trust must be shared.*
- *Truth fits like duck's foot in mud pond.*
- *Two lovers in moonlight cast only one shadow. One shadow now—many shadows later.*
- *Under strong generals there are no weak soldiers.*
- *When friend asks, friend gives.*
- *Woman's tongue like sword that never gets rusty.*

Princess Ming Lo Fu Lullaby

Princess Ming Lo Fu is the central character of a Chinese children's lullaby sung by Charlie Chan, in *Charlie Chan in Shanghai* (1935). After playing a game of leap frog on the deck of an ocean liner sailing to Shanghai, a young Chinese girl asks Chan if he would sing the song about Princess Ming Lo Fu. This film is the only time in the entire series that Charlie Chan actually sings. The lyrics of the song are as follows:

> *"Long the journey on the way, but his heart was gay,*
> *For was he not the Prince both strong and brave,*
> *But the Princess fair to save.*
> *And he slew the mighty dragon, even cut off his seven heads,*
> *And in his cave he found the Princess bound to her lowly bed.*
> *Then came they both back to the land of the mighty Emperor Fu*
> *   Manchu,*
> *To claim his reward, the dainty hand of lovely Ming Lo Fu."*

1935 Pennsylvania Referendum

An unusual short film is that of Warner Oland in the character of Charlie Chan who lobbies in support of a 1935 referendum in Pennsylvania to allow theaters to show movies on Sundays.

"Biggest mysteries are not always crimes. Most mysterious is what mankind does to itself for reasons difficult to understand. For instance, Eskimo will not eat meat of seal in certain seasons even if starving. Men in India will go barefoot on hot coals to prove devoutness. South sea islanders may not smoke before grandfather. African tribesman put painful sticks through nose to be beautiful, and his lady love stretch neck like ostrich to be more beautiful. And in honorable state of Pennsylvania, populous will not permit itself to enjoy motion pictures on Sunday. Old proverb say, strange laws make even more strange bedfellows! Humble self very much puzzled why one man may play golf game on Sunday and other man cannot see Charlie Chan bring criminal to justice on same day. Respectfully suggest, you use mighty power of ballot on fifth day of November to remove unnecessary obstacle to innocent pursuit of pleasure. Thank you so much!"

Peter Lorre as Mr. Moto

Mr. Moto is the mild-mannered Japanese detective who was the basis for a series of eight films (1937–1939) by Twentieth Century Fox from the stories of novelist John P. Marquand. Peter Lorre portrays Kentaro Moto, who was much unlike Charlie Chan in that he was the master of disguises and physically more active, often using ju-jistsu.

Peter Lorre (1937-1939)

Mr. Moto Filmography

Think Fast, Mr. Moto (1937)

Thank You, Mr. Moto (1937)

Mr. Moto's Gamble (1938)

Mr. Moto Takes a Chance (1938)

Mysterious Mr. Moto (1938)

Mr. Moto's Last Warning (1939)

Mr. Moto in Danger Island (1939)

Mr. Moto Takes a Vacation (1939)

Think Fast, Mr. Moto (1937)

Peter Lorre . . . . Mr. Kentaro Moto
Virginia Field . . . . . . Gloria Danton, alias of Tanya Boriv
Thomas Beck . . . . Bob Hitchings
Sig Rumann . . . . Nicolas Marloff
Murray Kinnell . . . . Joseph Wilkie
John Rogers . . . . Carson
Lotus Long . . . . Lela Liu
George Cooper . . . . Muggs Blake
J. Carrol Naish . . . . Adram
Fredrick Vogeding . . . . Curio dealer

- *A beautiful girl is only confusing to a man. (Bob Hitchings)*

- *Half the world will spend its time laughing at the other half —and both are fools. (Bob Hitchings and friends)*

- *Love is very tiresome for a third party. (Bob Hitchings)*

- *Patience is the most useful of virtues. (Lela Liu and Joseph Wilkie)*

- *When modern people cling to convention, there's always a purpose. (Bob Hitchings)*

Thank You, Mr. Moto (1937)

Peter Lorre . . . . Mr. Moto
Thomas Beck . . . . Tom Nelson
Pauline Frederick . . . . Madame Chung
Jayne Regan . . . . Eleanor Joyce
Sidney Blackmer . . . . Herr Eric Koerger
Sig Rumann . . . . Colonel Tchernov
John Carradine . . . . Pieriera
William Von Brincken . . . . Schneider
Nedda Harrigan . . . . Madame Tchernov
Philip Ahn . . . . Prince Chung
John Bleifer . . . . Ivan

• *Birth is not a beginning; death is not and end. (Prince Chung)*

Mr. Moto's Gamble (1938)

Peter Lorre	Mr. Moto
Keye Luke	Lee Chan
Dick Baldwin	Bill Steele
Lynn Bari	Penny Kendall
Douglas Fowley	Nick Crowder
Jayne Regan	Linda Benton
Harold Huber	Lieutenant Riggs
Maxie Rosenbloom	Horace "Knockout" Wellington
John Hamilton	Philip Benton
George E. Stone	Jerry Connors
Bernard Nedell	Clipper McCoy
Charles Williams	Gabby Marden
Ward Bond	Biff Moran
Cliff Clark	Tom "Mac" McGuire
Edward Marr	Sammy
Lon Chaney, Jr.	Joey
Russ Clark	Frankie Stanton
Pierre Watkin	District Attorney
Charles D. Brown	Scotty, editor

- *To recognize one's faults requires intelligence; to admit them requires courage. ("Knock-out" Wellington)*

- *Much information can obtained from tongues loosened by anger. (Lt. Riggs)*

- *I have often noticed that the dog an the human are very much alike. Each will go to any length to obtain something he desires, or to destroy something he believes dangerous. (Gabby Marden)*

- *The usual way to avoid trouble is to lock it out. I lock it in. (Lt. Riggs)*

- *To reveal a snake, one must overturn a rock. (Lt. Riggs and the District Attorney)*

- *Some people save strings. I pull them. (Nick Crowder)*

- *In poker, the man with the poorer cards very often wins on a bluff. (Lt. Riggs)*

Mr. Moto in Danger Island (1939)

Peter Lorre	Mr. Moto
Jean Hersholt	Sutter
Amanda Duff	Joan Castle
Warren Hymer	Twister McGurk
Richard Lane	Commissioner Gordon
Leon Ames	Commissioner Madero
Douglas Dumbrille	Commander La Costa
Charles D. Brown	Col. Thomas Castle
Paul Harvey	Governor John Bentley
Robert Lowery	Lieutenant George Bentley
Eddie Marr	Captain Dahlen
Harry Woods	Grant

- *One cannot gain the confidence of criminals unless one is branded a criminal. (Twister McGuirk)*

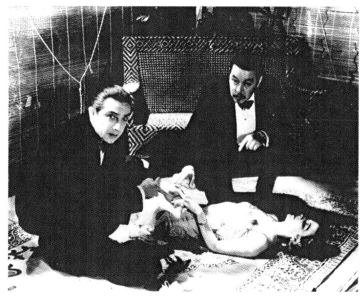

Béla Lugosi and Warner Oland kneel over the dead body of Dorothy Revier in a scene from *The Black Camel*.

Sidney Toler and Joseph Crehan examine a murder chair in a scene from *Black Magic*.

Harold Huber, Donald Woods, Keye Luke, Warner Oland in a scene from *Charlie Chan on Broadway.*

Warner Oland and Mark Garrick set up a dummy in front of a cabin room window as a trap in a scene from *Charlie Chan Carries On.*

Sidney Toler asks to examine Douglass Dumbrille's ring with Sen Yung looking on in a scene from *Castle in the Desert*.

Some of Charlie Chan's "Multitudinous Blessings" in a publicity shot from *Charlie Chan's Greatest Case*.

The entire Chan family of 12 children in a scene from *Charlie Chan at the Circus* with Warner Oland at far right and Keye Luke third from left.

Weldon Heyburn, Joan Woodbury, and Sidney Toler in a scene from *The Chinese Cat.*

Warren Douglas, Louise Currie, Roland Winters in a publicity still from *The Chinese Ring*.

Warner Oland shares tea and doughnuts with circus midgets George and Olive Brasno in a scene from *Charlie Chan at the Circus*.

Gilbert Emery (left) and E.L. Park, the screen's third Charlie Chan in a scene from *Behind That Curtain*.

"The desert gives and the desert takes" says Boris Karloff in his first talkie role to Warner Baxter in a scene from *Behind That Curtain*.

Emmett Vogan, Sidney Toler, Joe Allen, Jr., Gloria Warren, Dick Elliot, Rick Vallin, over the dead body of Tristram Coffin in *Dangerous Money.*

Teala Loring, George Holmes, Sidney Toler, and Benson Fong in a scene from *Dark Alibi.*

Warner Oland and Thomas Beck discover the key to opening a secret room in Ahmeti's tomb in a scene from *Charlie Chan in Egypt*.

Boris Karloff, Nedda Harrigan, and Warner Oland in *Charlie Chan at the Opera*.

Eugene Borden, Leo G. Carroll, Sidney Toler, and Harold Huber in a scene from *City in Darkness*.

Howard Negley, Carol Forman, Roland Winters, and Emmett Vogan in a scene from *Docks of New Orleans*.

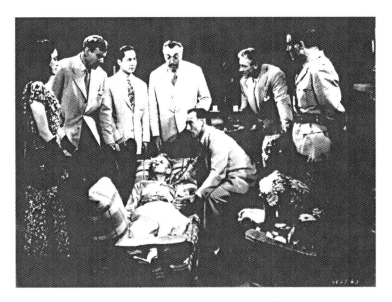

Carol Forman, Nils Asther, Keye Luke, Roland Winters, Robert Livingston, George J. Lewis, Erville Alderson (on couch), and Juan Duval (doctor) in a scene from *The Feathered Serpent*.

Sen Yung, Jack La Rue, and Sidney Toler in a scene from *Charlie Chan in Panama*.

Warner Oland performs a chemical test for murder clues in a scene from *Charlie Chan's Secret*.

Arthur Loft, Gwen Kenyon, George Lewis, and Sidney Toler in a scene from *Charlie Chan in the Secret Service*.

Sidney Toler, Douglas Fowley, Pauline Moore, and Cesar Romero in a scene from *Charlie Chan at Treasure Island*.

Roland Winters and Milton Parsons in a scene from *The Shanghai Chest*.

Lightning Source UK Ltd.
Milton Keynes UK
UKOW04f1157300114

225557UK00001B/215/P

ISBN: 1-58715-469-2

$14.99 U.S. / $20.99 CAN

BRYAN D. SIMS

LEADING
TOGETHER

THE HOLY POSSIBILITY OF HARMONY AND
SYNERGY IN THE FACE OF CHANGE

FOREWORD BY ALAN HIRSCH AND RICH ROBINSON